With relevant ıl,
succinct prose, ır
heart, and beck th
of the Lord. I was and ıd
profound insights. She has a gift for painting beautiful word
pictures that draw the reader in immediately. You will be
richly blessed by being In the Company of God.

- Cynthia Heald
Author of *Intimacy with God*
and the *Becoming a Woman of* Bible study series

In the Company of God is a spiritual oasis. Its truths,
eloquently written, cause me to pause and ponder the wonder
of being loved unconditionally by my Creator. It refreshes,
renews, and restores my passion for Him.

- Grace Fox
Co-Dir. of Intl Messengers Canada and author of
*Moving from Fear to Freedom: A Woman's Guide to Peace in
Every Situation.*

In her new book *In the Company of God*, Pam Teschner has
painted a picture that puts the reader into the company of
God. The reader will be able to better connect with the
doctrinal truths presented through the picture Pam develops
with her writing style. This book appeals to both a sense of
art and the longing of the heart.

- Dr. Mark A. Hoeffner
Exec. Dir. CB Northwest and Teaching Elder
Grace Church, White Salmon, WA

Pam has a great ability to relate God's heart and Truth to real
life. This devotional is theologically rich, honest, tender and
easy to read. The God-focus gives me a solid rock of
assurance for the day as I read each devotional.

- Barbara Fletcher
Associate Pastor, Salem Alliance Church

This gem of a devotional book ushers one into the company of God. The invitation to contemplation breathes through the carefully selected Scripture passages, and the accompanying reflections from Pam Teschner's holy attention to God's presence.

- Susan S. Phillips, Ph.D.
Exec. Dir. of New College Berkeley and author of
Candlelight: Illuminating the Art of Spiritual Direction.

My soul was drawn in immediately, wanting more of the Savior! Pam's words are carefully carved out of her own heart. She knows pain. She's experienced God in the midst of pain. Integrating the words of Scripture with Pam's incredible ability to paint pictures with words results in an experience that potentially is life-changing. The reader senses she/he is walking on sacred ground--invited into intimate places with Jesus. Take time with each reading--to let it fully penetrate your soul. And you will likely find yourself returning daily.

- Bev Hislop, D.Min.
Assoc. Professor of Pastoral Care
Exec. Dir., Women's Center for Ministry
Western Seminary

These beautiful encouragements offered by Pam Teschner will help her readers walk closer to God.

- Colette Tennant, Ph.D.
Professor of English, Corban University

Pam Teschner reveals much about herself in this book, but, more importantly, she reveals much about her God. Through trials, changes and a great variety of circumstances, Pam has learned that God *is* in control and that His ways are so much better than any alternatives.

- Ellen Kersey
English and Journalism, Corban University

IN THE COMPANY OF GOD

My dear cousin,

How special to see you!

God wraps His love around

you and sings over you.

Pam Teschner

Yet I still belong to you;
you are holding my right hand.

You will keep on guiding me with your counsel,
leading me to a glorious destiny.

Whom have I in heaven but you?
I desire you more than anything on earth.

My health may fail, and my spirit may grow weak,
but God remains the strength of my heart;
he is mine forever....
as for me, how good it is to be near God!

Psalm 73:23-26, 28a
NLT

How very good it is to be in the company of God.

IN THE COMPANY OF GOD

PAM TESCHNER

ISBN-10: 1466324333
ISBN-13: 978-1466324336

Cover design: Renee Barratt
Pencil sketches: Pam Teschner

Printed in the United States of America

To
the women of First Baptist Church
of Brownsville, Oregon
for whom this book is written.
Thanks for the inspiration.

And to
Heirborne, my pack of friends and confidants who
prayed and prayed and prayed:
Cathy Nelson
Debbie Shanks
Denice Lee
Dixie Kearns
Jamey Suderman
Jennifer Bertz
Marcy Shanks
Rhonda Atchley
Thanks for surrounding me with your prayers.

CONTENTS

ACKNOWLEDGMENTS

God's orchestration of every detail of this process has astounded me. In his perfect timing, He planted a dream within me then aligned people and events to make it a reality.

David Sanford, this would not have happened without your guidance and encouragement. You opened a door of possibility and led me by the hand to a place I never imagined.

Colette Tennant, your edits and suggestions made my writing so much better than it would have been without your touch. You smoothed out many rough edges.

Renee Barratt, you created just what I had envisioned for the cover. I'll always remember that cool April morning at the Oregon Garden when God brought you across my path. And, thanks Susan for inviting me along.

Debbie, our many years of friendship and the uncountable hours we spent pondering God are reflected in these pages. You lived much of this with me and opened my eyes many times to the wonder that is God. Thanks for trekking around lakes, up mountains, meandering through the forest, along the beach and paddling up the river. But mostly for staying by my side through the dark valley and lifting my face to behold God.

He has done immeasurably more than all my imaginations. To God be all glory and praise!

INTRODUCTION

In the stillness of pre-dawn darkness, 12 disciples slept. Amid the usual chorus of snores, Jesus woke and pondered the day ahead. He sighed from the weariness of His body, then rose and slipped on His robe and sandals. He stretched and nearly tripped over a lumpy blanket.

Through slitted eyes, John watched his friend slip through the door. It had become a predictable routine over the past couple of years. Occasionally, he followed, but this time was different. He sensed a need for solitude in his friend and stayed under the blanket.

Jesus loved to watch the spreading light of sunrise illuminate the stark beauty of the desert. Finding a large rock to sit on, He faced east and moved the earth to bring the first ray of light over the mountains. He smiled remembering the day He spoke the sun into the sky. A breeze rustled the dry grasses and a desert lark greeted his Maker. Tiny tracks of a rodent disappeared in the flurry of wing prints in the sand. He caught the movement of a sluggish lizard crawling into the warming light. The creature seemed to be reveling in its own renewing moment.

The desert was a place of solitude that Jesus enjoyed with His Father. Each knew the thoughts and the heart of the other. Great joy flowed between them in the early morning hours of the Judean desert. They were united in perfect love that stretched from age to age and everlasting to everlasting.

Jesus prayed for His sleeping friends and for their faith and oneness. He prayed for those who loved Him and those who hated Him. He prayed for the pious religious and the rejected poor. And He prayed for those teetering on the edge of belief. He looked across the coming centuries at all who would follow and prayed for you and for me.

Today He waits for me in solitude. When I rise in weariness of body and sit with Him, He is near. Some days, I'm swept up in the overwhelming joy of Deity. Some days, I hang my head in silence waiting for a movement of the Sovereign God. Some days, I doze off. But, thankfully, He is always attentive to me and will gently stir my soul with peace and hope.

I don't understand why the Eternal God would be arrested by my sigh and stoop to my lowliness. I don't understand it, but He waits for me to come to Him.

My heart has heard you say, "Come and talk with me."
And my heart responds, "LORD, I am coming."

Psalm 27:8
NLT

That God Himself wants a personal conversation with me is beyond my capacity to comprehend. Even more incredible is His longing for my companionship. All too often His voice is drowned out by my furious flaps of busyness. But when I fold my wings and remain before Him in stillness, my heart will hear the deep whisper of the Eternal God... *"Come and talk with me."*

Sometimes I regard His invitation lightly and hurry through my day. But my soul weakens and grows thin when I neglect Him or give Him short shrift. Spending solitary time with Jesus Christ is a discipline of urgent necessity. He doesn't extend a casual "if you have time" invitation. He extends an imploring cry out of the depths of His soul... *"Come and talk with me."*

By His design, there is no depth of relationship without heart conversation. The prayers of the Psalms are the pulse of the soul and give voice to the heart. They run the gamut of raw unfiltered emotion shouted from the mountaintop of praise and whimpered from the deepest pit of despair. They juxtapose our human condition with His supremacy and tenderness.

Psalm 119 reverberates with David's love and hunger for the word of God over and over and over again. Then, as a finale, David laments, *"I have strayed like a lost sheep. Seek your servant, for I have not forgotten your commands." (vs.176)* We are so fallible and so prone to wander from the Maker and Savior of our souls. Driven by His deep desire for our companionship, Jesus tirelessly and endlessly seeks His strays.

As I stray in a desert of doubt, I wonder what's the point. In my heart of hearts, I know it is this: I so desperately need Him to be Lord of my life, my choices, my thoughts, my words, my work, my relationships...absolutely everything. I need to see Him in the tedium of my days and in the world that drains me. I need to hear His voice above the cacophony and chaos or I will be swallowed by it. I need to be in such union with Him that His life replaces mine.

I am just dust…frail, fallible and swept away by doubt. But when I fail, my Father remembers that He made me dust and is deeply moved with great love and tender compassion. Then my heart hears Him say, *"Come as you are, spend some time alone with me and talk with me."*

LORD, I am coming!

O GOD, You are my God; early will I seek You;
My soul thirsts for You; my flesh longs for You
In a dry and thirsty land where there is no water.

Psalm 63:1
NKJV

Let the morning bring me word of your unfailing love,
For I have put my trust in you.
Show me the way I should go,
For to you I lift up my soul.

Psalm 143:18

CHAPTER ONE

STEPPING STONES

You were shaped and formed out of love too vast to comprehend. God Himself invites you to walk with Him and tell Him all the details that press your heart. He seeks the same union with you that He enjoys with His Son. Everyday He calls to you and, even at this moment, He tugs at you to meet Him in the secret garden of your soul.

Do you know that the great longing of the great heart of God is for intimate friendship with you? Your heart was made to be locked in perfect oneness with the heart of the Living God. The door to sweet intimacy with God will swing open with the key of faith and the breath of a prayer.

Stepping stones of promises are scattered along the garden path, and the air is heavy with the fragrance of His love. Breathe deep and linger long. Walk with Him in the cool of the evening, in the freshness of the morning and throughout your day. Lean upon Him and listen. In the quiet of the garden, the trickling sounds of His love will saturate your soul and satisfy your deepest longings. You will revel in His strength and be overcome with His peace and irrepressible joy.

You have made known to me the path of life;
you will fill me with joy in your presence,
with eternal pleasures at your right hand.

Psalm 16:11

CHAPTER TWO

RHYTHMS

The Eternal God chose me and set His love upon me before I was born. He numbered my days of breath before setting the earth upon its foundation. Eons later, at exactly the perfect moment, I was conceived, and He began weaving together all the delicate complexities of my body one cell at a time.

He wrote my genetic code on submicroscopic DNA molecules unique from every human He has made and ever will make. He formed muscle, bone, and nerve tissue all from two original cells. In a mere few weeks, the gentle pulse of Deity nudged my tiny heart to beat. Billions of brain cells coalesced into a thinking, feeling, learning, creating mind.

The trilogy of grace, love and forgiveness were sung over my heart in a rhythm flowing out of ages past giving life to my gasping soul. God wrote my story before my first breath and has been orchestrating every step of the journey to the very last step. One day my eyes will close for the final time but will open in that same moment to see Him face to face on the other side.

.

*You made all the delicate, inner parts of my body
and knit me together in my mother's womb.*

*Thank you for making me so wonderfully complex!
Your workmanship is marvelous — and how well I know it.*

*You watched me as I was being formed in utter seclusion,
as I was woven together in the dark of the womb.*

*You saw me before I was born.
Every day of my life was recorded in your book.
Every moment was laid out
before a single day had passed.*

*Psalm 139:13-16
NLT*

CHAPTER THREE

GLENEDEN BEACH

The pulse of rolling waves relentlessly sweeps over the sandy beach. The mounting wave becomes translucent green streaked white. The growing force pulls and lifts brown sand, coloring the inside curve of the wave. It crests white, then curls over in a roar of boiling foam. Fleeting rainbows appear in the salty spray of the crash. The shoreline gives it voice as it surges and breaks over sand and rock. Foamy white lace decorates the surface of the wave as it runs up the beach. Thirsty sand drinks up the edges of the spreading wave as it reaches, then recedes back to the sea. Scattered tufts of froth skitter down the beach, blown by the wind.

Day after day, month after month, year after year the sea relentlessly flows over the beach. Undone by the power of the sea, the sand is lifted, stirred and rearranged. Slowly the beach is shaped and transformed by the power of the sea.

Relentlessly, the power of the love of God sweeps over me. It surges toward the shoreline of my soul and crashes upon it. Wave after wave of His love surges over my soul, undoing it, lifting it and transforming it. The power of His love cannot be contained or restrained as it washes over me. It never rests and never ceases in its pursuit of the shaping of my soul. Mine is but to lie still and drink up the edges of the spreading wave.

The LORD reigns, he is robed in majesty;
the LORD is robed in majesty and is armed with strength.
The world is firmly established;
it cannot be moved.

Your throne was established long ago;
you are from all eternity.

The seas have lifted up, O LORD,
the seas have lifted up their voice;
the seas have lifted up their pounding waves.

Mightier than the thunder of the great waters,
mightier than the breakers of the sea —
the LORD on high is mighty.

Deep calls to deep
in the roar of your waterfalls;
all your waves and breakers
have swept over me.

Psalm 93:1-4; 42:7

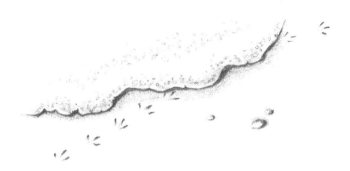

CHAPTER FOUR

WINGS OF THE WIND

O Sovereign LORD, no existence in heaven or earth compares with You. My mind is overwhelmed by the infinite depth of Your greatness. The limitless cosmos declares Your glory. How can I be silent surrounded by a symphony of praise?

You are the Great Sovereign of the past, the present and the future. In this moment You inhabit both the beginning and end of time. You orchestrate every day toward the final establishment of Your kingdom. Ah, Lord God, there is none like You!

One day the trumpet will sound and every eye of the living and the dead, even those who pierced You, will see you riding on the wings of the wind and shining more brilliant than the sun. All the people over all the earth from Alaska to South Africa will see You and will fall on their faces.

O Sovereign LORD, who am I that You care so much for the smallness that is me? I am but faithless dust blown by the winds of time and, yet, I am Your treasure.

Praise the LORD, O my soul.

O LORD my God, you are very great;
You are clothed with splendor and majesty.

He wraps himself in light as with a garment;
He stretches out the heavens like a tent,
And lays the beams of his upper chambers on their waters.

He makes the clouds his chariot,
And rides on the wings of the wind.

He makes winds his messengers,
Flames of fire his servants.

He set the earth on its foundations;
It can never be moved.

Psalm 104:1-5

CHAPTER FIVE

CONTEMPLATING INFINITY

Consider the great love of the Lord.
Psalm 107:43b

Wrapping my mind around the love of God is like trying to contemplate infinity. It's like peering deep into the star-studded night sky, and imagining endlessness. To consider the great love of God is to ponder the eternal uncreated Existence before the beginning…before earth…before stars and space dust…before angels…before everything. A brief flicker of eternity illuminates the darkness of my mind for an instant, and my soul gasps at the fleeting light. My mind reaches to describe it, but it vanishes beyond words and paradigms. The vastness of eternity somehow resides within my being and is etched upon my soul.

The immense ocean of His love floods and overflows my small heart. It swells with the unimaginable fullness of His love until, enraptured and overwhelmed, it nearly bursts. This is but a modicum of His love, and if I should glimpse its complete fullness, I would perish in the crush of its glory.

Every fiber of the Eternal God stretches out after me. Before everything, He chose me and called me to Himself. He intends me to experience the indescribable joy of His Presence in the innermost core of my soul -

His heart beating within mine, and mine within His. That kind of love is far too weighty for my puny mind to grasp.

He relentlessly pursues this mortal bundle of bones with all its failings and is satisfied with nothing less than every cell of it. He knocks at the door of my heart gently but persistently. Hearing His voice, I fuss about attempting to tidy up the disarray of my heart to make it fit for the King's entrance. Embarrassed and ashamed, I try desperately to clean out the dust and dirt of life. Hard as I might, I can't shake it off my feet but continue tracking it through the rooms of my heart.

In complete poverty of spirit and trembling faith, I crack open the door of my disheveled life. In utter amazement, I am swept up and enveloped by God Himself. Glory dawns over my soul. In that moment I know I am His and He is mine…no matter what.

I will praise you, O LORD, among the nations;
I will sing of you among the peoples.

For great is your love, higher than the heavens;
your faithfulness reaches to the skies.

Be exalted, O God, above the heavens,
and let your glory be over all the earth.

Psalm 108:3-5

CHAPTER SIX

PEARLS

In days past, my spirit was overwhelmed and wounded. I was crushed to the ground and shattered. Dreams of careening through blackness haunted my sleep. But in all my anguish and distress, He, too, was distressed. He spread His protective wings over me and rested me near His heart. Again and again He whispered…*"Wait on me."*

God's healing balm began to form around the object of pain. Slowly and almost imperceptibly, a marvelous pearl miraculously began to form in the pit of the wound.

> I found the strength of God
> When I lost all strength.
> I found the heart of God
> When mine lay in pieces.

> When my soul was wracked with pain,
> I found the unfailing compassion of God.
> When dark clouds obliterated the day,
> I found the light of the world dawning in my soul.

The enemy pursues me,
He crushes me to the ground;
He makes me dwell in darkness like those long dead.

So my spirit grows faint within me;
My heart within me is dismayed.

I remember the days of long ago;
I meditate on all your works
and consider what your hands have done.

I spread out my hands to you;
My soul thirsts for you like a parched land.

Psalm 143:3-6

CHAPTER SEVEN

CAPTURED

Sometimes it's the gentle breeze of His Spirit
That arrests my attention.
Sometimes it's His whisper in the trees.
And sometimes it's the first ray of sunrise touching my
Face as it breaks gloriously over the mountains.
Then my spirit sighs, captured once more by His love.

I love You, O Lord, my strength.
Words are too small for what my heart holds.
They are dwarfed next to Your cross.
Fill this heart with more and more of Your love
And I will pour every drop of its fragrance over You.

I love you, O LORD, my strength.

Psalm 18:1

CHAPTER EIGHT

EMBERS

I wish I were more immediate in my confession of sin. Instead, I tend to minimize or rationalize it. But the longer I cover it up, the deeper it descends into my spirit. Hoarded sin darkens my eyes and casts a chill over my heart. The flame of spiritual vitality dims and cools. Over time, unconfessed sin sinks into my bones and saps my strength.

God is so willing and so wanting to cleanse and restore me. But my will flies off like a howling hound down a path of selfishness. Unceasing relentless footsteps match my every turn in His pursuit of me. Weary from running, I finally turn toward Him and find myself wrapped in His waiting arms.

Have mercy on me, O God! Wash the grime of the world off my wandering feet. Cup Your hands around the faint embers of my heart and breathe it into a blazing flame of worship. Fill me with the thirsty passion of Your Spirit until I'm utterly lost in the deep wonders of Your love.

When I kept silent,
my bones wasted away
through my groaning all day long.

For day and night
your hand was heavy upon me;
my strength was sapped
as in the heat of summer.
Selah

Then I acknowledged my sin to you
and did not cover up my iniquity.
I said, "I will confess
my transgressions to the LORD" —
and you forgave
the guilt of my sin.

Psalm 32:3-5

CHAPTER NINE

MARYS PEAK

Marys Peak, at 4,097 feet, is the highest point of Oregon's coast range. The peak is a perfect place to witness the hand of God move the earth. On a clear day, the Pacific Ocean is visible to the west and snow-capped peaks of the Cascades to the east.

One day in late summer, my friend and I made the trek to the top. Noble fir and spruce lined the trail winding to the summit. The coast range stretched north and south, mountain after mountain, in lightening shades of bluish purple.

At that elevation the breeze is chilly, so we hunkered down in the dry grass to watch the sun slowly inch toward the western horizon. The shadow of the peak we were upon crept slowly across the Willamette Valley to the east. The green and brown patchwork of farmland grew darker. Lights of the towns below glittered like diamonds scattered over the floor of the valley.

A couple with a small boy sat on a blanket upslope from us. Several young couples came around the bend and stood on the path below. More and more people began to congregate on the top of the mountain to watch the spectacle...drawn by Someone much larger than themselves.

As the sun touched the horizon, everyone grew quiet as if on cue. Couples moved closer together, riveted on the unfolding beauty and changing colors of the sunset. The little boy chattered behind us, but was gently hushed by his mother. We all watched in mesmerized silence as the horizon slowly swallowed the sun. Awe from the human soul was palpable. A holy moment touched the peak. Then, as the last point of light disappeared, dusk settled over the earth.

God, who breathed out stars and spoke the world into existence, brought another day to an end. On the opposite side of the planet, the sun rose and His mercies began afresh once again. Let all the people of the earth stand in awe of the God who holds this planet in His hand and carries it around the sun.

By the word of the LORD were the heavens made,
their starry host by the breath of his mouth.

He gathers the waters of the sea into jars;
he puts the deep into storehouses.

Let all the earth fear the LORD;
let all the people of the world revere him.

For he spoke, and it came to be;
he commanded, and it stood firm.

Psalm 33:6-9

CHAPTER TEN

REFERENCE MARK:
MARY 1940

One fall day in 2004, I knelt in the dirt next to a reference mark and, with paper and pencil, created a rubbing of the surface. As I rubbed the pencil lead back and forth over the paper, words began to emerge as white letters defined by graphite. It was "Mary," a reference mark set into the rock on the south side of Marys Peak in 1940 by the National Geodetic Survey.

Reference marks like Mary are drilled deep into a stable foundation at high elevations such as mountain peaks or on high towers. Surveyors use these critical points of reference to determine true position, location and distance. From the height of the mountain, relationships and distances in the valley are much clearer.

As I muddle along the valley floor of life, I'm easily overwhelmed and my perspective becomes distorted. I become ant-like exploring the millimeter in front of me with outstretched antennae, lost in the forest of the insignificant. But from the heights, I see beyond the little space I occupy and beyond the giant problems that tower around me. My point of view shifts to the expanse outside of myself, and I see my true position in Christ.

The unchanging monolith of Truth is a reference mark set deep into the Rock. Coming back to this critical point of reference, I catch a glimpse of the panoramic vista of the love of Christ – the width, length, height and depth of it. And I see the wisp of life disappearing into the vanishing point on the horizon of eternity.

From the end of the earth I will cry to You,
When my heart is overwhelmed;
Lead me to the rock that is higher than I.

My soul, wait silently for God alone,
For my expectation is from Him.

He only is my rock and my salvation;
He is my defense; I shall not be moved.

In God is my salvation and my glory;
The rock of my strength, and my refuge, is in God.

Psalm 61:2; 62:5-7
NKJV

My name is permanently engraved upon the rock of salvation and sunk deep into the immovable and unshakeable heart of God. Likewise, His name and His seal are irrevocably stamped upon my soul and He delights in me with great joy. That is truth and simply grace.

CHAPTER ELEVEN

NEVER FORGET

O my soul, never forget His grace nor from where you have come. My base nature is against God and stinks of death. It steps around the filth and grime of humanity and seeks praise to assuage its insecurities. My nature rises in anger when my rights are not served and is defensive when accused. Its tongue is sharp and quick to lash out in criticism. It stands on Smug Hill above those with less.

My nature is undisciplined and casual with grace. It turns away from the crucified Christ, repulsed His disfigured body. His groans no longer hurt my heart but fade into my own self-absorption. So, I move through my busy day without falling on my knees in complete wonder and utter amazement that He would even turn His face toward me and gift me with another breath.

Yet, the heart of Jehovah yearns for His child with great compassion. He embraces me with gentle grace and looks upon me with tender affection. He sets His love and compassion upon my soul as a crown. Then He lavishes me with abundant grace and fills my heart with all it could ever desire…immeasurably more than I could ever ask or imagine!

O my soul, never forget His mercy. I deserve nothing less than an eternity in hell, but He does not treat me as my sins deserve. Instead, He unleashed the fierce fury of His wrath upon His Son and my Sin-bearer. He killed His Son to redeem me from the pit of hell. My futile attempts to live the Christian life as He requires demean His sacrifice. How could I dare presume myself capable of even the smallest act of righteousness or deserving of even the smallest measure of His grace? My nature thinks it must try.

Praise the LORD, O my soul;
all my inmost being, praise his holy name.

Praise the LORD, O my soul, and forget not all his benefits —

Who forgives all your sins and heals all your diseases,
Who redeems your life from the pit
and crowns you with love and compassion,

Who satisfies your desires with good things so that your youth is
renewed like the eagle's.

The LORD is compassionate and gracious, slow to anger,
abounding in love.
He will not always accuse, nor will he harbor his anger forever;
He does not treat us as our sins deserve or repay us according to
our iniquities.

For as high as the heavens are above the earth,
so great is his love for those who fear him;
As far as the east is from the west,
so far has he removed our transgressions from us.

As a father has compassion on his children,
so the LORD has compassion on those who fear him;
For he knows how we are formed, he remembers that we are dust.

Psalm 103:1-5, 8-14

CHAPTER TWELVE

FULL OF COMPASSION

The voice of His child stops God in His tracks. A small desperate hand reaching for Him will capture His attention and His heart. Even as a weak breath is drawn, He has already turned with great compassion and tender care. Stooping, He leans His ear to the lips of His struggling child.

There was a time when my voice was swallowed by an emotional storm that howled around me as my marriage collapsed. Overcome and nearly undone, I cried out for my Father. He turned His ear to me and stretched Himself out to the fullest taking hold of my sinking faith. With kindness and great compassion, He lifted me and carried me over the waves.

In every storm, despite the depth of its darkness or its furious force, there is this hope for His child: God is faithful, and He is still on the throne. Because of His great love and unfailing compassion, He will not let the fury consume you but will carry you through it. Then one day, He will command the storm to pass. In its aftermath, His gift of faith will lay exposed by the waves and be stronger because of the tempest.

God may seem asleep in the stern of your little boat as it's buffeted, but He is in control. He doesn't always speak peace to the storm, but He always stands upon the waves and speaks peace to the heart.

I love the LORD, for he heard my voice;
he heard my cry for mercy.

Because he turned his ear to me,
I will call on him as long as I live.

The cords of death entangled me,
the anguish of the grave came upon me;
I was overcome by trouble and sorrow.

Then I called on the name of the LORD:
"O LORD, save me!"

The LORD is gracious and righteous;
our God is full of compassion.

The LORD protects the simplehearted;
when I was in great need, he saved me.

Be at rest once more, O my soul,
for the LORD has been good to you.

Psalm 116:1-7

CHAPTER THIRTEEN

CLEFT OF THE ROCK

I can almost hear Moses pleading, *"If you are pleased with me, teach me your ways so that I may know you…."* And I can almost feel the tenderness in the voice of Jehovah, *"I will do the very thing you have asked, because I am pleased with you and I know you by name." (Exodus 33:13, 14)* Moses could not bear taking another step without Him. Such passion moved the heart of Jehovah in a very personal way.

All too often we become lulled into a dull stupor moving mechanically through life. We've lost the passion to know Him. Worse, we delude ourselves into thinking we can move from day to day by our own plans and perseverance. We keep Jehovah in a dusty box and forget about Him. Yet still He says, *"I am pleased with you and I know you by name."*

Moses approached the fearsome display of God's power with insatiable hunger. He placed His life in the hands of Omnipotence and cried out in desperation to know Him and to see His glory.

It is an awesome frightening thing to freefall into the hands of Almighty God. But those who dare to *really* trust Him and cry out for His glory will be astounded by His immense Goodness.

Lord, set me in the cleft of the Rock
Where I can feel the radiance of Your glory,
Hear the thundering pulse of Your power
And know the tender protection of Your hand.

O Most High, proclaim Your Name
Until it shakes the foundation of my soul.
Loosen the stones my hands have laid without You.
Then cause Your Goodness to fill
The opened spaces with veins of gold.

The one thing I ask of the LORD —
the thing I seek most —
is to live in the house of the LORD all the days of my life,
delighting in the LORD's perfections
and meditating in his Temple.

For he will conceal me there when troubles come;
he will hide me in his sanctuary.
He will place me out of reach on a high rock.

Psalm 27:4-5
NLT

CHAPTER FOURTEEN

SIDE STREAMS

Paddle harder! Paddle harder! That's all I could hear as I strained and puffed and paddled against the current of the Willamette River. The tour guide for the kayak paddle was yelling and waving me over toward the left bank where the Luckiamute River joined the Willamette. The current attempted to pull me farther away, but finally I maneuvered into the quiet side stream.

Compared to the fast pace of the Willamette, the little tributary was serene and beautiful. Trees lined the banks and hung over the river. I drifted under leafy branches, absorbing the tranquility and inhaling the fragrance of green. After a time of rest, I paddled back into the current and went on with the day, refreshed and renewed.

The crazy current of life with its activities and demands sweeps me along its routine. As life goes on, it seems to grow faster and broader with responsibilities. The voice of my Guide calls me to come away and follow Him into the quiet side streams. If I don't purpose to set all my strength to follow Him, I'll be swept downstream, pulled along by the relentless demands of life. And doing nothing just carries me farther from where He wants me to be.

Paddling against the current of responsibilities to spend time with Christ is a discipline, an act of obedience. Many mornings, heaven seems silent and my room empty. But still I pray and wait because He wants to hear the sound of my voice. Even a wordless sigh of my heart captures His attention.

There's something unique about meeting Him in the early morning hours and starting the day with Him. Yet I let the wild current of life pull me away from the One who loves me most. This God of mine waits for me every morning, and every morning His compassions are brand new. He waits to lavish me with His grace all over again.

Slipping into the quiet side stream of His presence, the fragrance of His compassions and His peace envelop me. After a time of soaking Him up, I paddle into my day with grace lingering upon my mind and spirit.

Give ear to my words, O LORD,
consider my sighing.

Listen to my cry for help,
my King and my God,
for to you I pray.

In the morning, O LORD, you hear my voice;
in the morning I lay my requests before you
and wait in expectation.

Psalm 5:1-3

CHAPTER FIFTEEN

GRACE BROKE THROUGH

We tend to bury our sin under the covers of well-intentioned lives and consider it less than the disgusting sins of others. After all, how awful is worry or a small lie compared to rape and murder? Our social system ranks sin and punishes the perpetrator as befits the crime. But in the kingdom of God, even the "least" of my sins sentences me to complete destruction.

Sometimes sin takes the shape of self-pity and pain-clinging. I'm wronged and cling to the hurt, but slowly and secretly a mass of life-draining roots sneak into the crevasses of my heart. In the vague depth of my soul, a quiet groaning misery weakens my spirit.

Clutching pain and brooding over hurts are far easier than giving it to God. In my pain and fear and muddled heart, my prayers hesitate and fall silent. Who knows what He might do or ask me to do?

When I refused to confess my sin, I was weak and miserable,
And I groaned all day long.

Day and night your hand of discipline was heavy on me.
My strength evaporated like water in the summer heat.

Finally, I confessed all my sins to you and stopped trying to hide
them. I said to myself, "I will confess my rebellion to the LORD."
And you forgave me! All my guilt is gone.

Psalm 32:3-5
NLT

Forgiveness is hard. Grace is harder. But how can I, who have been forgiven much, not forgive? How can I, so lavished with the riches of His grace, not be a grace-giver? If I have not grace in my heart, then grace does not have me. So, I confess my pain-clinging and grace floods my heart.

Oh, what joy for those whose rebellion is forgiven,
Whose sin is put out of sight!

Yes, what joy for those whose record the LORD has cleared of sin,
Whose lives are lived in complete honesty!

Psalm 32:1- 2
NLT

And, oh what terrible, terrible sorrow when grace is not received. How it must hurt God's heart when His extended grace is left in His scarred hand. The gift cost Him everything.

CHAPTER SIXTEEN

QUIET STRENGTH

We stand upon a 6.6 sextillion ton magnet suspended in emptiness. God holds it as a speck of dust and orients its position in space and the direction of its tilt to perfectly sustain life and create the beauty of seasonal change.

The free hanging needle of a compass swings in response to the earth's magnetic force. The metal of the needle is made up of tiny miniature magnets, each with its own north and south poles. The magnetic strength of the needle increases as all the north and south poles align. If the needle were hit, the miniature magnets inside would be knocked out of alignment and become a random jumble, neutralizing the strength of the needle. The needle, too weak to point north, is unable to give any direction to the lost.

Something amazing happens if the weakened needle is rubbed against a strong magnet or sticks to it for a long period of time. The tiny magnets all askew will begin to align and orient themselves with the strong magnet. The longer the weak needle stays close, the stronger it becomes.

The day-to-day struggle to survive knocks my soul out of alignment with the power of Christ. I feel jumbled up and out of synch with Christ. A nagging wrongness and unsettledness pervades my thoughts and trips my steps. I've gone my own way and haven't spent time alone with Christ. This separation has left me with a sense of randomness and spiritual disorientation. I've become too weak to point to Christ or give any direction to the lost.

Behind the jumble, God whispers, *"In quietness and trust is your strength." (Isaiah 30:15)* As I rest in complete trust near the strength of His heart, my spirit and my will slowly begin to align with His. His transforming power gradually reorients my core. The more time I spend near Him, the stronger I become until a song slips from my lips…

O, my Strength…O, my loving God.

But I will sing of your strength,
in the morning I will sing of your love;
for you are my fortress,
my refuge in times of trouble.

O my Strength, I sing praise to you;
you, O God, are my fortress, my loving God.

Psalm 59:16-17

CHAPTER SEVENTEEN

COURSE CORRECTION

A small spacecraft launched into space will keep going along the path of its original trajectory as long as no other force intervenes. The craft will maintain the same speed and same direction unless the gravitational pull of a larger object shifts it off course or it's knocked off course in a collision.

Once the path shifts, it will keep going along the shifted path. Over time, the spacecraft will get more and more off its intended course. Even a few subtle degrees of shift will cause it to get off its designed path and completely miss its intended destination.

Mission Control watches and monitors the progress of the craft. When it gets off course, Mission Control will use a course correction to get it back on the right path. The current location, speed and direction of the spacecraft are calculated to determine where it is compared to where it should be. A new vector is computed, and Mission Control fires the craft's small attitude rockets, changing the direction it's pointing. Then the main attitude thruster is fired to push it along the right path.

Like spacecraft, we've been launched into life and along a path of God's design. Sometimes bad stuff crashes into us and we wander off in a daze. Or the irresistible force of temptation lures us into a place far from God. The shift may not be noticeable today or tomorrow or next week. But over time, we've divided our time and our pursuits and have strayed farther and farther off course. One day we realize, to our horror, that we're somewhere we never intended to be. All the while, God has tracked every step and knows our precise location. With great love, He continually seeks to restore us and nudge us back on the right path with a little attitude thruster.

Unless I purpose every day to set my heart undivided before God and walk in His truth, I will be an easy target for attack. I do not want to find myself years down the road having missed His best.

Teach me your way, O LORD;
lead me in a straight path because of my oppressors.

Psalm 27:11

Teach me your way, O LORD, and I will walk in your truth;
give me an undivided heart, that I may fear your name.
I will praise you, O Lord my God, with all my heart;
I will glorify your name forever.
For great is your love toward me;
you have delivered me from the depths of the grave.

Psalm 86:11-13

CHAPTER EIGHTEEN

FINGER OF FAITH

At the end of a Sunday worship service, God surprised me with an extraordinary moment. I stood on the platform playing bass with the worship band as people milled around after the service. The melody of *"What the Lord Has Done in Me"* filled the sanctuary while the crowd talked and greeted each other.

> *Let the weak say, "I am strong."*
> *Let the poor say, "I am rich."*
> *Let the blind say, "I can see."*
> *It's what the Lord has done in me.*

A mother and her young daughter, making their way down the middle aisle, caught my eye. Mom waited at the bottom of the three steps to the platform while the little brown-haired girl climbed the steps.

She was transfixed, and her big brown eyes saw nothing but the rough-hewn cross that stood at the side of the platform. It was draped with a white cloth, and a crown of three-inch thorns hung on the crossbeam. Her face glowed with innocent wonder and awe as she stepped up to the cross. Pensively, she reached up on tip toes and gently touched a thorn. Time and sound were suspended as I watched.

Into the river, I will wade.
There my sins are washed away,
From the heavens mercy stream
Of the Savior's love for me.

At the foot of the cross, a little finger of faith touched Love. I'm certain Jesus was standing near and smiled. The air was electric with His Presence. Satisfied, she turned and walked down the steps. Mother and daughter melted back into the noisy crowd and drifted away.

Hosanna, hosanna
To the Lamb that was slain
Hosanna, hosanna
Jesus died and rose again.

Jesus, restore to my heart wonder and praise that transcends the trappings and complexities of grown-up life. May I reach a pensive finger of faith to touch Your thorns.

Praise the LORD from the heavens,
praise him in the heights above.

Praise him, all his angels, praise him, all his heavenly hosts.

Praise him, sun and moon, praise him, all you shining stars.

Praise him, you highest heavens and you waters above the skies.

Praise the LORD from the earth, you...
kings of the earth and all nations,
you princes and all rulers on earth,
young men and maidens, old men and children.

Let them praise the name of the LORD,
for his name alone is exalted;
his splendor is above the earth and the heavens.

Psalm 148:1-4, 7, 11-13

CHAPTER NINETEEN

RUNNING BY FAITH

One day as I was running, I noticed two men about a block ahead running shoulder to shoulder in lockstep. The runner on the left had his right hand on the forearm of the runner next to him. I realized the one on the left was blind and running by faith. He was running in the dark and couldn't see the path, but he trusted and held on to the one at his right hand. He trusted each of his steps to the one next to him who saw the path ahead and knew every pitfall. He did not lift his hand from his guide or head off on his own. He simply followed by faith.

I managed to get closer and see their faces as they turned a corner. There was no look of concern or panic on the face of either runner. I could tell they had spent much time running together. The blind runner knew he could completely trust His sighted companion.

There is a disadvantage to sight - I trust too much in my eyes and don't feel the need to trust when the way is treacherous. I have been trained to walk by sight and trust only what I can see. Yet, God asks me to run by faith and not by sight.

Running by faith is a deliberate commitment to the faithfulness of Jesus Christ and holding on to Him even when I can't see the way ahead. He knows the pitfalls and will never lead me astray. When I go my own way, I stumble. When I trust Him to lead me, I will not be shaken, for He's always at my right hand.

I have set the LORD always before me.
Because he is at my right hand,
I will not be shaken.

Show me your ways, O LORD,
teach me your paths;
guide me in your truth and teach me,
for you are God my Savior,
and my hope is in you all day long.

Psalm 16:8, 25:4-5

CHAPTER TWENTY

PURSUIT OF HAPPINESS

Echoing waves of unimaginable delight roll through the cosmos. At the epicenter, God Himself sings and rejoices over His children with great joy. He *is* unbounded joy, and He designed us to be filled to the brim and overflowing with it.

Because of our Creator, an insatiable hunger for happiness gnaws at the core of humanity. We insist on the right to happiness and spend our lives pursuing it. The Declaration of Independence establishes the self-evident truth that we have all been endowed by our Creator with certain inalienable rights, including the pursuit of happiness.

So, we pursue happiness in things, experiences and relationships. In pursuit of "happily every after," we spend our lives accumulating wealth, toys and lovers. We lap at puddles of shallow affections with our backs to an ocean of exquisite joy.

Worldly happiness vanishes at the first hint of trouble, but the joy of God sustains and imbues the heart with strength. It underpins the ebb and flow of life's sorrows. It endures beyond the end of life and carries us into eternal pleasures.

Why does this happiness seem like a wisp of mist vanishing the moment things heat up? Why am I not overflowing with joy all the time? Perhaps, deep down, I think I've disappointed Him and He will never be able to forget my failures. Mostly, I think I'm just not quite good enough yet. So, I stand at a distance, afraid I'm right.

Gently, He coaxes me out of hiding. Tentatively, I move closer, incredulous of His love but so wanting to believe it. As I get closer, His fountain of pure joy begins to well up in my soul unbidden. A realization suddenly overwhelms my restraint. God is rejoicing over me…just as I am right now! Even when I completely mess up and make foolish mistakes, He still rejoices over me because I am His and His alone.

Praise the Lord!
Sing to the Lord a new song,
Praise Him in the assembly of His saints!

For the Lord takes pleasure in His people;
He will beautify the humble with salvation
And adorn the wretched with victory.

Let the saints be joyful in the glory and beauty
[which God confers upon them];
Let them sing for joy upon their beds.

Psalm 149: 1, 4, 5
AMP

.

CHAPTER TWENTY-ONE

MAYFLIES

There was a day some years ago that I sat in the hollow of a rock on the banks of the S. Santiam River. I was at a significant crossroads that altered the course of my life. After having custody of my two sons for four years, I had just given up custody to their father. The decision to let go was agonizing, but God-directed. I sat watching the translucent green water swirl and flow by, disappearing around a bend downstream. The rustling leaves of the cottonwoods on the opposite bank gave voice to the soft breeze. The September sun blanketed me in warmth, but a crushing emptiness gripped my heart.

After a time, I looked closer at the rock I was leaning against and saw the shed skins of mayfly nymphs attached to the rock all around me. They had crawled out of the water onto the same rock I had crawled onto and rested there to complete their metamorphosis. They transformed and emerged completely different creatures, then flew away. All that was left on the face of the rock was the fragile empty skin of their past.

I sat on the rock afraid of what was around the next bend, but God asked me to shed the empty skin of fear. It is a very hard thing to let go and trust Him with one's sons. But my hope is in God, and He has already written the next chapter and the next and the next.

Why are you downcast, O my soul?
Why so disturbed within me?

Put your hope in God,
for I will yet praise him,
my Savior and my God.

Psalm 42:11

And what a blessing, a few years later, when both of my
sons came home.

CHAPTER TWENTY-TWO

INTO THE DEPTHS

My words just skip and bounce over the surface of a great deep if they are not of You, O God. Bring me to the end of skimming the top, and sink me into the infinite depths of Your heart. Think through me. Pray out Your heart in me. Put Your words in my mouth, or the words will not be worth saying.

My soul pants with longing for more of You. I need to see You and hear You in the monotonous shallows of life. Reveal Yourself to me and open my eyes to Your Presence. I want to see what no eye has seen, hear what no ear has heard and know what no mind has conceived. Let me hear the deep melody of Your boundless love, and I shall sing it back to You!

As the deer pants for streams of water,
so my soul pants for you, O God.

My soul thirsts for God, for the living God.
When can I go and meet with God?

Psalm 42:1-2

CHAPTER TWENTY-THREE

A ROAD WELL TRAVELED

God travels upon the road of my life and planned every step I would take before I was born. It winds through lonesome valleys and climbs the precipice of steep mountains. He is my Companion and will never leave me stranded or abandon me on the road.

A difficult mountain looms ahead; my steps falter. I'm hesitant to follow as He ascends. Over the years, I've faced a number of ominous mountains including the loss of my marriage, letting go of a career, the death of my father, financial struggles, graduate school, difficult relationships, moral choices, health issues and the list goes on and on.

Looking upon the dizzying heights of the mountain, I can't bring myself to let go of absolutely everything and put my life in His hands. In choosing my own path around the challenge, I wander dangerously close to the edge. What seems to be an easy way around leads to a long plunge onto the jagged rocks of sin. As I step away, Christ moves protectively close to keep me from falling. Then He gives me grace to trust and follow Him up the mountain.

He knows when I need a respite from the demands of the climb and leads me through lush green meadows and beside still waters. He provides these oases to restore my soul and give me courage to take another step.

But there's an experience on the heights of difficulty that can never be found in the meadow. The narrow path of the mountain pass forces me closer to Him than on the open meadow. On the precipice of a mountain there's a deeper bonding of spirit and unique intimacy with Christ. Were it not for the difficulties and struggles, I would not know Him as I do.

Whether through mountains or meadows, there are refreshing springs and pools of blessing around every corner of the road well traveled. But they are discovered only when following in the footsteps of Christ. The hollows left by His footprints fill and overflow with glorious blessings for those who follow.

And how blessed all those in whom you live,
Whose lives become roads you travel;

They wind through lonesome valleys,
Come upon brooks,
Discover cool springs and pools brimming with rain!

God-traveled, these roads curve up the mountain,
And at the last turn – Zion!
God in full view!

Psalm 84:5-7
MSG

CHAPTER TWENTY-FOUR

PARADISE RESTORED

The paddle dips right, then left, right, left in a slow relaxing rhythm under the warm sun. With each dip, silver whirlpools spin in the translucent green water. Paddling up a lake tributary, serenity engulfs my spirit. This is paradise on earth…a remnant of Eden.

Tall Douglas fir and broadleaf maple line the shore, creating a meandering corridor of green. Thick moss carpets crooked branches of the maples. Sunlight turns its leaves into patterns of luminous yellow and dark green. Fir bows tipped in the light green of new growth stretch out over the tributary. Old man's beard lichen hangs from aged trees in long grey-green hairy strands.

Here and there, large boulders jut up from the waterline, creating a sense of open sky cathedrals. Sunlight reflected from the water dances on the grey stone surface. Blue-green sedum, corals and moss cover the rocks. Small ferns peek out of cracks and crevices in the fractured surfaces. Out from the shore, a sunny boulder sticks its head above the waterline, proudly displaying a magnificent hairpiece of grass, daisies and purple wildflowers.

Two eagles soar in the brilliant blue sky high overhead. As they turn, head and tail feathers flash white in the sunlight. Another bird of prey is on the wing nearby, and I look for the characteristic white patches on the underside of its wings. The cry of the osprey captures me and stirs my soul.

Rounding a bend, a mother duck and two ducklings come into view. Mom swims leisurely along, while the two small ducklings paddle furiously behind. Fuzzy yellow motor boats leave tiny V wakes as they speed along after mom. One meanders off, clapping his bill onto some tasty morsel he discovered on the surface. A quack from mom and the peeping little motorboat soon catches up.

The growing brightness of the sun moves over the page of my scribbles as I drift from shade to sun. As the page brightens, I soak up the warmth. A few feet from my kayak, a salamander lazily surfaces, gulps a breath of air, then undulates back into the green depths. A tell-tale bubble rises to the surface behind him. A June bug buzzes and a noisy Kingfisher swoops over the water, then perches in a nearby tree, chattering and squawking at my intrusion. A small iridescent blue dragonfly investigates my red kayak, and a swallowtail butterfly flutters up and down on the breeze, curious about the strange creature in a straw hat.

In this piece of paradise, my Lord and I have delighted in each other's company. He took great pleasure in showing me His art and smiled at my joy.

There is nearly always a head wind when paddling out of paradise. It's as though God isn't anxious for me to leave and would have me linger longer.

The LORD is my shepherd;
I shall not want.

He makes me to lie down in green pastures;
He leads me beside the still waters,
He restores my soul.

Psalm 23:1-3a
NKJV

CHAPTER TWENTY-FIVE

IN THE COMPANY OF GOD

Imagine a face-to-face encounter with Almighty God! I can't conceive what Moses experienced in that kind of conversation with his friend Jehovah. Or grasp the joy of Eve as she strolled through the garden with God smiling and laughing at her side.

You and I were made for companionship with Almighty God and to experience the joy of the reality of His Presence. Do we have the desperate desire of Moses to know God more fully? How often do we plead with the same depth of passion for the company of God? Have I spent time today face to face with God, enjoying His companionship?

Admittedly, I take His Presence for granted far too many times and rush off like I'm in charge of my day. But, how lonely it is when I shut the door to His nearness and visit with Him only at my convenience.

God Incarnate, who walked the earth and stands at the right hand of the throne of God, who will come again and reign as King of kings and Lord of lords, seeks my companionship from the bottomless depths of His heart. He wants to speak with me as with a friend and know me face to face.

He can be as real to me as He was to Eve…even more because He actually lives inside me! He is closer than my very breath. Even as I write those words, I can't grasp the full import of that statement. I walk in the company of the One who shakes mountains and whose holiness leaves a trail of blinding glory behind Him.

Sometimes I'm senseless and stupid. *Yet* I am always and continually in the company of no less than Almighty God Himself! The statement is not preceded by the conditional *if*…if I am faithful…if I don't fail him…if I'm perfect. It is preceded by *yet*…yet I am always with You in spite of my failures and foolishness.

Walking daily with Jehovah is a transforming experience. I begin to resemble Him as I spend more and more time near Him, talking with Him and listening to Him. His thoughts begin to pervade my thoughts, His words begin to form in my mouth, and His love begins to pour out of my heart. I hear the whispers of His Spirit within me, guiding me and praying for me.

Since my conception and birth, He has carried me and sustained me. I can never fall out of His hands, and He will never cast me off even when I'm worn out and raggedy…not even when I'm grumpy.

One day I will hear the rustle of wings, and He will carry me home to live forever in the company of God.

I was senseless and ignorant;
I was a brute beast before you.

Yet I am always with you
You hold me by my right hand

You guide me with your counsel
And afterward you will take me into glory.

Psalm 73:22-24

CHAPTER TWENTY-SIX

CROSSROADS

None of us pass through this life unscathed. At some point, we will be pierced by a wrong and stand at a crossroads. The course of our lives will be set by what we choose at that critical juncture.

Two paths diverge and lead in very different directions with very different destinations. The cross stands dead center in the path of forgiveness. The pilgrim of forgiveness embraces the cross and finds healing and freedom. But the road of resentment leads to captivity and hardness. The insidious root of bitterness bores into the spirit and contorts the countenance. It sends its deadly tendrils into every crevice of the heart and bleeds it dry.

I have stood before a crossroads of deep hurt, and struggled taking the first steps. The cross loomed ahead, and soon I stood eye level with the bloody feet of Jesus. Looking up the length of His brutalized body, I saw the ravages of sin. He became every wrong, every obscenity of humanity and every heinous crime. Then He paid the debt with His life. There is no sin so great that He will not forgive.

Human nature screams retribution, but the Spirit of God whispers forgiveness. Our humanness hangs on to the hurt and drags around the dead body of the past.

Eventually we become chained to the past and cannot grasp the future.

Forgiveness breaks the chains and frees the soul. It is not a feeling but a choice of obedience. It does not wait for apologies or repentance and is not contingent upon sincerity. It embraces the one who wronged us with the forgiveness of Jesus Christ.

Forgiveness does not change the past or erase the consequences of bad choices, nor does it always repair broken relationships. It does not minimize the hurt or stop the pain, but it lays the aching heart and broken pieces in the wounded hands of Jesus and trusts Him to do a healing work. I have learned that forgiveness is a long journey of giving the wrong and the hurt to God…again and again and ever again.

Some time ago, I ran across a little red notebook I had tucked away. I knew it was time to let go of the penned past and burn pages and pages of awful memories. With the heat of the fire warming my face, I watched memories turn to black ash. A sense of finality and freedom settled into my soul as the fire died. In time, a crown of beauty and blessing rose from the ashes. There comes a time when we must purge the memories of the past to find the freedom of the present and grasp the goodness of the future.

We all arrive at your doorstep sooner or later loaded with guilt,
Our sins too much for us –
But you get rid of them once and for all.

Blessed are the chosen!
Blessed the guest at home in your place!
We expect our fill of good things in your house,
Your heavenly manse.

Psalm 65:3-4
MSG

CHAPTER TWENTY-SEVEN

COLORS OF MY SOUL

Clear quartz crystals, black basalt, amber agates, and an occasional grain of green olivine are illuminated in the light of my microscope. Peering through the lens, I examine tiny details of each grain of beach sand. My fingers turn the fine focus knob to search out each glint of color, each edge and each crevice of each grain. No two are alike. Each is weathered into a unique shape by the winds and rains and pounding waves.

All the grains of the sand of my soul are sifted through the fingers of God. He peers into the depths of my heart, carefully searching out the tiny details of my life. Each glint of color, each edge and each crevice of my heart are intently examined by God. He has uniquely shaped me by the winds and rains and pounding waves of life to create the many colors of my soul.

There is nothing about me – no movement, no word, no feeling – that He doesn't know completely and intimately. He knows every thought and intent of my heart and unearths what I have so carefully hidden. In fact, He watched me bury it.

There's nothing that He doesn't already know about me. He knows and has always known my past and my future. He knows my deepest darkest secrets and loves me no less and no more than infinitely. There is nothing to hide from a love that never cools even by the slightest degree. I am completely and irretrievably secure in the everlasting love of God.

He is beside me as I sleep and watches me rise and hurry through my day. He is the unwavering companion at my side through the course of my journey, in front of me to lead the way and behind to protect me. There is never a moment that I am outside of His gaze. His eyes are fondly fixed on me, His ear is ever bent toward me, and His hand…his great loving hand…is upon my soul.

This is incomprehensible. It's too high for me to grasp. I couldn't in a lifetime know the depth of God's tender care for me. There is nothing in the finite realm to measure the All-Knowing. So, I sit in wordless wonder.

O LORD, you have searched me
and you know me.

You know when I sit and when I rise;
you perceive my thoughts from afar.

You discern my going out and my lying down;
you are familiar with all my ways.

Before a word is on my tongue
you know it completely, O LORD.

You hem me in — behind and before;
you have laid your hand upon me.

Such knowledge is too wonderful for me,
too lofty for me to attain.

Psalm 139:1-6

CHAPTER TWENTY-EIGHT

PRIVATE CHAMBER

Through the west door off the White House Oval Office is the President's private inner sanctum. Presidents have used it as a quiet retreat to be alone in their thoughts and relax. Only those closest to the President are allowed inside. So, it's not likely that I would ever be allowed to sit with the President of the United States in his private office. Security would tackle me before I could even get close.

I may not be known by the President, nor do I ever expect to be invited into his private quarters, but there is One of much higher power and authority that knows me by name and has invited me into His private chamber. He reigns as High King over all kings and rulers.

At one time the private chamber of the Most High God was closed off by a thick veil suspended from ceiling to floor. It was the Holy of Holies – so sacred only the high priest could enter and only once a year carrying the blood of the sacrifice.

When Jesus died on the cross for our sins, God tore the veil and opened a way into His most secret place. Our sins previously barred us from entering, but He made a way for us by His blood. He opened Himself to us and exposed His innermost sanctum as an invitation to enter.

He wants us to come near and live in close companionship with Him. He made the way; now, it's up to us. We can be as close to God as we choose to be.

It is a rare experience to sit in the mysterious place of the Shekinah glory of the Most High God. All too often we dash in and dash out, too busy and self-possessed to stay there. We are completely oblivious to the hush of holiness in that place.

Even still, God reaches out as we rush by. He desperately longs for our company. He yearns for us to sit down with Him, talk with Him and just hang out with Him. Great grace and unimaginable blessings are reserved for the few dwellers of the inner chamber.

In times of trouble, the one who dwells in the secret place of the Most High will pass the night under the protective shadow of Almighty God. There is no deeper rest.

He who dwells in the secret place of the Most High
Shall abide under the shadow of the Almighty.

I will say of the LORD, "He is my refuge and my fortress;
My God, in Him I will trust."

Surely He shall deliver you from the snare of the fowler
And from the perilous pestilence.

He shall cover you with His feathers,
And under His wings you shall take refuge;
His truth shall be your shield and buckler.

Psalm 91:1-4
NKJV

CHAPTER TWENTY-NINE

THE GREAT SPRING

As a teenager trying to find my way through Christianity, my dad said to me, "Sis, all you need to do is keep the debris clear from your life and the Spring of Living Water will fill you and flow through you." That truth has stayed with me and became very real to me when I stood at the headwaters of the McKenzie River.

A deep subterranean river springs out of the ground and flows into a small pool, then into Clear Lake. The spring is known as The Great Spring. The force of the flow originates at the roots of the Cascade Mountains above Clear Lake and flows downward, seeking open channels.

For thousands and thousands of years the water has flowed continually into Clear Lake, then down the mountain on its journey to the Pacific Ocean. Turquoise water of the McKenzie churns white as it rushes over rocks and under dripping ferns.

The crystal clear icy water of the spring pours through open channels in the dirt and gravel along the edge of the pool. One hot summer day, I took off my shoes and socks and dipped bare feet into the aching cold water. It was one of those gasping moments. I reached down into one of the holes as far as I could and felt the force of the water pushing and welling up from deep underground. I cleared away some rocks and debris to make the hole larger and allow even more water to pour through. I was struck at how the water flowed so deliberately through the holes. I didn't have to draw it out. It poured through the openings by another force. And it will flow day and night for years to come.

The debris of sin and self-effort blocks the flow of water and stagnates my life. All I need to do is confess my sin and the unending flow of the irrepressible life of God will fill me to overflowing. His boundless life will well up in my soul as the Spring of Living Water without end.

*Have mercy on me, O God,
according to your unfailing love;
according to your great compassion
blot out my transgressions.*

*Wash away all my iniquity
and cleanse me from my sin.*

Psalm 51:1-2

Flow through me oh mighty river!
Wash away all my sin and flood me
with Your very own life.

CHAPTER THIRTY

THE SECRET

If I am not experiencing supernatural joy in spite of my circumstances, if I am not growing closer to God, if I keep tripping up on the same sins, then I am not where He intends me to be.

If I want to change from the inside out, if I want to stop sinning so much, if I want the blessings of God on my life and my relationships, then He is ready to open the flood gates of blessings.

The secret is simple but difficult. It requires the discipline to step aside and disconnect from the world and enter the private rooms of God. We must stay connected to the flow of His life by opening the Word of God every day and reading it, memorizing it, praying it, speaking it out loud, pondering it, chewing on it and reading it again.

Over time, the joy and peace of Christ will begin to grow and blossom within our soul. He will transform us from the inside out, and we will begin to reflect His image with ever-increasing glory.

…and on his law he meditates day and night.
He is like a tree planted by streams of water,
which yields its fruit in season and whose leaf does not wither.
Whatever he does prospers.

I have hidden your word in my heart
that I might not sin against you.

I run in the path of your commands,
for you have set my heart free.

Great peace have they who love your law,
and nothing can make them stumble.

Psalm 1:2b-3; 119:11,16,32,165

You can take that promissory note to the vault of the riches of God.

CHAPTER THIRTY-ONE

BEGINNING AND END

The substance of all creation issues from God. He is the power generating megatons of energy every second from countless stars scattered across an endless universe. With a breath, the clouds swirl over land and sea. He grows crystal encrusted caves in the heart of the earth and feeds eaglets on rocky crags.

He is the Alpha and Omega, the Beginning and the End. He encompasses this sliver of time called earth history. It begins and ends within His infinity. For God, it is always the present. He IS now and yesterday and tomorrow. He is the past and the future in the present moment. I worry about the days ahead, but He is already there, leaving His footsteps for me to follow, then walks at my side into tomorrow.

My life is a nanosecond of eternity. Yet, all my days and years within that nanosecond are ordained and directed by the Sovereign God. For all the seconds of all my days, I will never be outside of His gaze and never separated from His love.

God, help me walk in company with You and live the fleeting moments of today in the overwhelming joy of Your Presence.

As for man, his days are like grass,
he flourishes like a flower of the field;

the wind blows over it and it is gone,
and its place remembers it no more.

But from everlasting to everlasting
the LORD's love is with those who fear him,
and his righteousness with their children's children —

with those who keep his covenant
and remember to obey his precepts.

Psalm 103:15-18

Selah

Pause and consider the One who has chosen you as His companion. Consider the One in whose company you are forever kept.

The LORD himself watches over you!

The LORD stands beside you as your protective shade
The sun will not hurt you by day,
nor the moon at night.

The LORD keeps you from all evil and preserves your life.

The LORD keeps watch over you as you come and go,
both now and forever.

Psalm 121:5-8
NLT

Go with God.

Additional copies of this book are available for sale online at:

www.CreateSpace.com
www.BooksaMillion.com
www.BarnesandNoble.com
www.Amazon.com

The author would love to hear from you.
You can write to her at pteschner@corban.edu.

Made in the USA
Charleston, SC
28 May 2013